A souvenir guide

Biddulph Grange Garden and Geological Gallery

Staffordshire

❀ National Trust

Biddulph Grange is one of the most exciting survivals from the great age of Victorian gardening. It is a commanding and confident showcase of flora gathered from the four corners of the world, during a time when one fifth of the Earth's surface was under Queen Victoria's rule.

James Bateman (1811–97) was a landowner, horticulturalist and one of the world's most respected orchidologists. Inheriting wealth accumulated through coal and engineering, he sponsored expeditions to Mexico and South America enabling collectors to gather rare specimens.

He published three books on orchids. Bateman commissioned artists to illustrate these lavish publications. One particularly fine example, *A Monograph of Odontoglossum*, contains thirty large-scale hand-coloured plates by Walter Hood Fitch (1817-92).

Bateman also had a passion for azaleas and rhododendrons, and to show his collection of exotic flora from all over the world to best effect, he developed a virgin site in the valley below Biddulph Moor in Staffordshire. Together with his wife Maria (1813–95) and their friend the marine painter and fellow gardener Edward Cooke, he built a new house and created an astonishing garden. But more than a garden, it was an exposition of all that was new and exciting in gardening as more parts of the world opened up to plantsmen and collectors.

Eclectic and eccentric

From 1842 and for over twenty years trees, shrubs and a wide variety of other plants were brought together at Biddulph Grange and set amongst rockwork, topiary, tree stumps and an extraordinary collection of eccentric garden buildings. The result is a series of spectacularly picturesque effects and varied microclimates, ranging from the exoticism of a Chinese 'willow pattern' landscape to the damp of a Scottish glen.

The gardens and the buildings exhibit the characteristics and ambitions of the Victorian age, as exemplified in the Great Exhibition of 1851 and the later recreation of the Crystal Palace at Sydenham: ingenuity and originality, variety and humour, technical innovation and surprise. They also reflect Bateman's belief in a 'designing God', a view that was prevalent in early Victorian society, but would be challenged most notably by the publication of Charles Darwin's *On the Origin of Species* in 1859.

Opposite
A gilded water buffalo sculpture looks out over China

Above left
James Bateman

Above
A Victorian orchid collector at work

Edward Cooke (1811–80)

In 1849 Edward Cooke paid the first of many visits to Biddulph Grange. The son of a distinguished engraver, Cooke was also the son-in-law of the nurseryman George Loddiges. At the age of nine he made drawings for *The Encyclopaedia of Plants* (1820) by the Scottish horticulturist John Claudius Loudon. He was also a Fellow of the Royal Geological Society.

Bateman's vision

Bateman was a noted botanist, a fellow of both the Linnean and Royal Societies and served as Vice President of the Royal Horticultural Society. He was fascinated by orchids, the 'master passion of his life', and he established a collection at the nearby family home, Knypersley Hall. Between 1837 and 1843 he published the largest book (in ten volumes) solely devoted to orchids, *The Orchidaceae of Mexico and Guatemala*.

James Bateman's passion for plant collecting coincided with the publication of a radical retake on the origins of life, with the result that botany and science and theology were brought together at Biddulph Grange to create something that would come to be much more than a garden.

Evolving beliefs

The mid-19th century was a time of great discoveries in the plant world and the gardens at Biddulph, with their 'created' microclimates, provided a showcase for the latest specimens collected by the great plant hunters.

But more significantly still, the garden and associated buildings at Biddulph Grange were constructed during a period when traditional and orthodox accounts of creation were being increasingly challenged by discoveries in science, in particular the findings of the fossil record and the intellectual developments which culminated in Darwin's theory on the origin of species and evolution.

Bateman, in common with many of his contemporaries, was a man of strongly held religious beliefs but he was also a brilliant botanist and a highly respected member of the scientific community of the time. In creating his 'world garden' he had the opportunity to allude to his beliefs and at the same time provide a showcase for his most-prized plant specimens. Amongst these were the golden larch, Japanese maple and other plants from the Far East collected by Robert Fortune, together with rare rhododendrons from the Himalayas brought back to England by Joseph Dalton Hooker. In the Pinetum, Bateman planted groups of specimen trees such as the deodar cedar and *Sequoiadendron giganteum*, commonly known as the Wellingtonia after the Duke of Wellington.

Bateman's centrepiece

The Geological Gallery is more than just a curiosity. It was central to James Bateman's vision and is a remarkable survival from an era of extraordinary developments in the new sciences and changing ideas on the world.

The ordering and layout found in the Geological Gallery are unique, reflecting Bateman's own belief in a designing God, and laid out in bays representing the days of Creation as described in the book of Genesis. It is the beginning of the story told by the whole garden – the dawn of time, through the days of Creation to the rise of successive civilisations represented by the various gardens.

Bateman's interest in geology was bound up in his horticultural endeavours, and the gallery provided a link to the variety of creation seen in a series of gardens representing different parts of the world. In the gallery Bateman expounded the diversity of creation illustrated by fossil remains through time, and beyond the gallery he represented the variety of creation by 'living fossil' specimens growing in the different conditions he had created in the various corners of his world garden.

James Bateman was resolute in his own belief in Divine Creation and in 1864 he wrote: 'To the believer, the problem is not hard to solve. Ferns and flowerless plants came early in the divine programme, because the coal into which they were ultimately to be converted, had need to be long accumulating for the future comfort and civilisation of our race; while the genesis of Orchids was postponed until the time drew near when Man, who was to be soothed by the gentle influence of their beauty, was about to appear on the scene.' Charles Darwin's theories of evolution were certainly unpopular with his contemporaries, amongst whom Divine Creation was the accepted truth, and roundly dismissed by many, but Bateman continued to correspond with him, supplying him with orchids and challenging his views in an open and scientific debate.

'Bateman has just sent me a lot of orchids with the *Angræcum sesquipedale*: do you know its marvellous nectary 11½ inches long, with nectar only at the extremity. What a proboscis the moth that sucks it, must have!'

Letter from Charles Darwin to J. D. Hooker, 30 January 1862

Above View from Day VI back to the dawn of time

Left Plates from *A Monograph of Odontoglossum:*
top
Odontoglossum grande
middle
Odontoglossum coronarium
bottom
Odontoglossum laeve

Far left *The Orchidaceae of Mexico and Guatemala* by James Bateman, *c.*1845. Only 125 copies of this, one of the largest botanical books ever published, were printed

Bateman's legacy

James Bateman developed and grew his remarkable garden at Biddulph over twenty years but, just as the passage of time documented in his walk-through gallery of life on Earth, there came a time when the garden too moved into a new era.

The splendour of Biddulph Grange required huge amounts of money and commitment. This proved for the Batemans to be an unsustainable passion and, defeated also by the damp Staffordshire weather, they left. In 1871 their son, John, sold the Biddulph Grange and Knypersley estates. They were both bought by a leading Staffordshire industrialist, Robert Heath, who maintained the gardens at Biddulph to a high standard and added further plants to the collections, especially hollies.

The present house at Biddulph Grange is largely a replacement of the earlier house and was built in 1896 by Heath's son following a fire that gutted the original Bateman house. However, the low wings of the original house and the Geological Gallery survived. In 1921, the last Robert Heath to live at Biddulph donated the house and estate for use as a hospital, and additional buildings were added to the site. The house continued to be used as a hospital until 1991, when it was sold. It is now in private ownership, having been converted into apartments. The National Trust acquired the gardens in 1988 and embarked on an extraordinary and extensive garden restoration project, returning Biddulph to the glory of its Victorian heyday.

Below An engine pumps water from the lake, while firemen and estate workers stand on the terraces. (The flames were painted in for dramatic effect.) Heath Family Album

The year in the garden

Spring

From early in the spring, the varied nature of Biddulph's gardens within a garden ensures that there is interest throughout the year.

In spring, the early bedding plants of the Italian garden are complemented by snowdrops in the Glen and the Woodland Terrace and by bluebells in the Pinetum. Throughout spring and early summer, the rhododendron display around the lake is one of the garden's main features.

The summer-time displays in Mrs Bateman's Garden are varied, reflecting the style in which they were originally planted, and in China the giant lilies flower in July. Scent from the bedding in Italy and the Verbena Parterre continues in the Rose Parterre. The highlight of the late summer is the dahlia display for which Biddulph is renowned.

Amongst the autumn highlights are the magnificent acers in China, the amber maples in the Arboretum and the beech hedge by Egypt.

In winter interest is held by holly and evergreens, as well as the extraordinary buildings and the sculptures that keep silent watch over the gardening team as they go about their work digging the dahlia beds, gravelling the paths, trimming and thinning the trees and ordering seeds for summer bedding.

Indeed, Biddulph Grange offers the visitor an experience unlike any other at any time of the year.

Autumn

Summer

Winter

The original entrance to the garden was through the Geological Gallery, with its extraordinary and interactive display of rocks and minerals. Today the Geological Gallery is the centrepiece of the restored garden (and also of this guidebook), the seed and the nucleus of James Bateman's creation, where developing science and orthodox theology came together.

However, before the main event, visitors to Biddulph Grange Garden can indulge all the senses on a journey through a number of very distinct areas, each with individual themes chosen by Bateman to celebrate and showcase his collected plants from far-flung places to greatest effect.

Italy
Rainbow

Opposite Italy viewed from the steps on the terrace. The borders on either side of the path are planted with annuals and Irish junipers in typical Victorian fashion

Below right A view from the terrace over a brilliant display of alternating rhododendrons and azaleas

Below left *Rhododendron roseum elegans*

Italy

Italian gardens became popular in Britain in the early 19th century. At first such gardens were based quite closely on Italian Renaissance examples, but by the time the Batemans came to design Biddulph, the label was applied more loosely to any garden with formally arranged flower beds, and usually featuring a stepped terrace and balustrades. Reflecting the classical tradition, this garden leads directly from the garden room, thus linking the house and the garden.

The borders on either side of the steps are planted in typical Victorian fashion with annuals bedded out. Other features are pairs of Irish junipers chosen to emulate Italian cypresses and deciduous species of late-flowering rhododendrons. Some of the rhododendrons have been replaced but others of the original plants have survived. The central circular stone trough is planted with golden yew.

Rainbow

Near the stone seat, designed by Edward Cooke, Bateman planted a feature he called the Rainbow. Rhododendrons and azaleas that would flower simultaneously were planted in distinct bands of colour on a semi-circular bank.

With equal ingenuity the Batemans aped the shadows cast by the pale green leaves of the limes by training dark green Irish ivy into scalloped shapes beneath them. Further back, groups of ivy and common box have been planted to form mound-shaped blocks.

Lime Avenue Rhododendron Ground

Lime Avenue

The Lime Avenue was once the highway between Biddulph and Congleton, and also served to link the vicarage that had stood on the site of the present house with Biddulph church. The avenue now ends in a fine set of gates, designed by Edward Cooke. Originally these were set at an angle to the end of the avenue. Beyond was a carriage drive through the former deer-park to the Batemans' other home, Knypersley Hall.

Rhododendron Ground

James Bateman was particularly fond of azaleas and rhododendrons, and he planted out the area around the lake with the limited range of species then available, and the early hybrids derived from them, together with other plants requiring acid soil. The first such plants came from North America – hence this area's other name, 'the American Garden' – although by the 1840s the term was being used more widely to describe a garden in which lime-hating plants from all over the world were grown. The rhododendrons here are mostly hybrids between hardy North American species and species from Turkey and Iran.

Here also is the first of the dramatic rockwork in the garden. Massive pieces of Chatsworth gritstone were brought down from the quarry at nearby Troughstone Hill and carefully arranged to suggest naturally formed outcrops. Heathers were also gathered from the moor, and weeping holly planted amid the rocks complete the effect. The island in the centre of the lake is planted with Kilmarnock weeping willows.

Left The Lime Avenue forms the western boundary of Biddulph Grange Garden. It predates the Batemans' arrival and the design of the rest of the garden

Right The Rhododendron Ground

Lake and lawns

Besides being the dramatic showcase of one of the most prolific and scholarly plant collectors of the 19th century, Biddulph Grange Garden was landscaped to provide the people who lived here and their guests a place for recreation and refined leisure pursuits, be it a punt on the lake or something more energetic on the manicured lawns.

Old Tennis Lawn

The Old Tennis Lawn was added by Robert Heath after James Bateman's departure and is surrounded by banks of azaleas and rhododendrons.

Bowling Green and Quoits Lawn

The smooth sward of the Bowling Green was reconstructed after excavations in 1988. This and the other informal lawns in this part of the garden are planted with a collection of tender, larger-needled South American pines underplanted with evergreens, shrubs and rose species.

Both the lawns and the lake were used for Edwardian recreational pursuits. Today you are welcome to take a turn about the well-groomed grounds or rest a while on one of the benches provided to enjoy the garden's tranquillity.

A Careful player. That'll do it Scotty

Quoits, little known today, was once a very popular pastime, with a centuries-old history and many variants. The outdoor, lawn version of the game involves the throwing of a metal or rubber ring over a set distance to land over a pin called a 'hob' or 'mott' in the centre of a patch of clay – the clay helps the quoit to stick in place once it has landed. The quoit is a circular disc that weighs anything up to 10 pounds (5 kg) with a four-inch hole in the centre traditionally made of steel. A quoit which lands on the hob is called a 'ringer' and scores two points. The first player to reach 21 wins the game. Players also try to land their quoits in ways which block further attempts by other competitors.

Far left From the lake you can strike out on a walk through some of the more open areas of the garden

Top left A game of mixed doubles. Heath Family Album

Bottom left A group setting out for a punt on the lake from the steps by the balustrade. Heath Family Album

Geological Gallery

The gallery is housed in a narrow two-storey building with a grand entrance at the western end opposite the main entrance to the house. It was originally the entrance to the garden. There was a waiting room to the north of the gallery, from which visitors were conducted through the gallery and out into the garden. The gallery is now accessed from the Woodland Terrace.

It is not certain when James Bateman began the gallery, but it was complete by 1862 when it was described in *The Gardener's Chronicle* (see over). Originally visitors were brought from a waiting room to the north of the gallery and through the porch at the west end of the building. The walls of the entrance porch were inset with architectural fragments and classical antiquities, probably collected by Bateman whilst travelling in Italy in 1835.

Charting the universe

In addition to these classical remnants, Bateman used the space to house his collection of geological and fossil specimens, organised in such a way as to illustrate the blueprint of the universe. Bateman's collection was organised in accordance with his belief in the biblical account of the seven days of Creation, with a series of seven bays each representing a geological epoch. The bays are marked with an inscribed stone corresponding to the days of Creation as described in the book of Genesis and explained by Moses in

Exodus 20:11: 'For six days the Lord made the heavens and the earth, the sea and all that is in them, but He rested on the seventh day. Therefore the Lord blessed the Sabbath day and made it holy.' In an enclosed space measuring just over 100 feet and representing time since the creation of the universe, two views are on show: that of the seven-day story contained in the scriptures that was the orthodoxy of Bateman's time, and the now generally accepted multi-billion-year account. Bateman's attempt to reconcile the two views is a bold one, but what this three-dimensional demonstration of intelligent design gives us is fascinating testament to the battle of beliefs that was being waged in the second half of the 19th century.

The fossil record

Biddulph Grange was in an area rich in fossil finds and mineral and rock deposits, and was also on the edge of a centre of industrial activity – mining for coal and iron ore, the burgeoning ceramics industry, road building, quarrying and canal construction. This activity uncovered fossil remains which Bateman would keenly collect. The fossils included trilobites and graptolites, Devonian fish, brachiopods and marine corals, dinosaur skulls and footprints, and even a mammoth tusk. Within Day III (representing the carboniferous period, see over for definitions of periods) were plant fossils, probably collected locally – the fossilised ferns, tree roots and mosses that provided the link to the 'living fossil' specimens Bateman grew in the gardens.

It is highly likely that Bateman and Cooke purchased some specimens from professional collectors like Mary Anning of Lyme Regis. One such fossil is a small and nearly complete ichthyosaurus with visible stomach contents. There were also examples of large polished spiral-shelled ammonites.

Bay VII was truncated in the 1930s when changes were made to the hospital and it is not known what was displayed here, but Bateman may have made some reference to the Garden of Eden, its human inhabitants and maybe his beloved orchids – 'The genesis of orchids was postponed until the time drew near when Man who was to be soothed by their gentle beauty was about to appear on the scene.'

Above **View along the Geological Gallery**

Left **Day III**

The Gardener's Chronicle, Edward Kemp, 1862

'The Geological Gallery, which is upward of 100-feet long, is lined with stone and lighted from the roof. Advancing into the gallery, it will be found treated in a way that is quite unique, and is singularly illustrative of the great facts of the globe. On one side, at about three feet from the ground, a series of specimens, showing the Earth's formation, and exhibiting all the various strata in their natural succession, are let into the wall, in a layer about eighteen inches wide; and above this are arranged the animal and vegetable fossils that the respected strata yield.... The whole is distributed into 'days' supposed to correspond with the six (so called) 'days' of Mosaic cosmology, beginning with the granites, and passing into the slates, the limestones, the old red sandstone, the coal formations, etc, with such animals and vegetable remains as occur in each.'

The geological periods

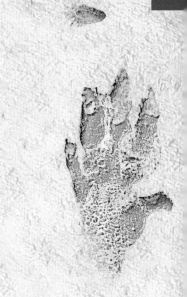

PRIMARY CHAOS, that saw Earth's creation, reckoned by scientists to be 4.6 billion years ago, also called PRE-CAMBRIAN

PHANEROZOIC ERA, from the 'appearance of life' (from the Greek 'phaino' [φαινω] and 'zoe' [ζωη]) to the present day, divided into:

PALAEOZOIC, from the Greek 'palaeos' [παλαιος] and 'zoe' [ζωη], meaning 'ancient life', 542–251 million years ago, in turn divided into:

Cambrian (542–488 million years ago) ⎤
Ordovician (488–444 million years ago) ⎬ Lower Palaeozoic
Silurian (444–416 million years ago) ⎦

Devonian (416–360 million years ago)

Carboniferous (also called Coal Measures, 360–299 million years ago)

Permian (299–251 million years ago)

MESOZOIC, 'meso-' [μεσο–] and 'zoe' [ζωη], 'middle life', 251–65 million years ago; used to be known as 'Secondary', in turn divided into:

Triassic (251–199 million years ago)

Jurassic (199–145 million years ago)

Cretaceous (145–65 million years ago)

CENOZOIC, 'kainos' [καινος] and 'zoe' [ζωη], 'new life', 65 million years ago to the present day; used to be known as 'Tertiary', in other words, everything that comes after 'Secondary'

Pinetum
Cheshire Cottage

Pinetum

After orchids, pines were James Bateman's great love. The Pinetum was laid out as a showground for one of the finest collections of conifers assembled in mid-Victorian Britain. He took considerable trouble to create a series of irregular mounds to show these trees at their best.

A tall, multi-stemmed coastal redwood towers over the Cheshire Cottage, while a fine Wellingtonia grows further along the Pinetum. Other important species include mountain hemlock (by the entrance to the Bowling Green), eastern hemlock and Japanese cedars. A group of swamp cyprus stands by an unusual variegated oak, its graft union – where the scion, or bud, is joined to the trunk – clearly visible. The medium-height planting consists mainly of holly and golden yew; low sweeps of heather, ivy, gaultherias and native ferns carpet the banks.

Left *Cedrus atlantica glauca*

Right Entrance to the tunnel to the Pinetum

Far left The Pinetum was created by James Bateman to provide the correct conditions of drainage, soil and shade for his beloved conifers

Left The Cheshire Cottage

Below A stone pinecone on the gates outside the Cheshire Cottage

Cheshire Cottage

The half-timbered Cheshire Cottage is really no more than a cleverly conceived façade, the fake timber frame no more than external battens set in plaster. The letters 'J & MB' commemorate James and Maria Bateman, '1856' the date of the cottage's construction. The stone pinecones flanking the path outside Cheshire Cottage announce a new theme in the garden – conifers.

Egypt

Egypt was one of the most original and distinctive of James Bateman's creations; it was also intended to be one of the garden's greatest surprises. Egyptian artefacts at the Great Exhibition and the Egyptian Courts at the Crystal Palace at Sydenham may have inspired its construction.

High hedges of beech and yew conceal a brilliantly theatrical design with two pairs of stone sphinxes guarding a hidden court, with obelisks of clipped yews standing in small, rectangular lawns. Ahead, stepped blocks of clipped yew topped with a pyramid form a topiary Egyptian temple. Beneath the topiary pyramid is a stone doorway with the symbol of Ra the Sun God above it, giving entrance to a dark passageway.

Below The Egyptian temple of topiary

At the far end of the passageway, in an unearthly ruby light, sits the Egyptian god Thoth, depicted as a man with the head of a baboon. Thoth was a scribe with mediating powers, the master of both physical and divine law. He was charged with making the calculations for the establishment of the heavens, stars, Earth and everything in them. The Greeks further declared him the inventor of astronomy, astrology, mathematics, geometry, land surveying, medicine, botany, theology, the alphabet, reading, writing and oratory. Straddling as Thoth does physical and divine ordinance, and credited with a hand in the creation of the universe and a leading role in the science of botany, he is an appropriate divinity and denizen of Bateman's Egypt.

The model for Thoth was possibly suggested by Edward Cooke, who in 1872 published *Grotesque Animals*, illustrated with even more bizarre creatures of his imagination. This book was written in response to Charles Darwin's discoveries about evolution, which disturbed both Cooke and Bateman. The ape was sculpted by Benjamin Waterhouse Hawkins, the creator of the life-sized dinosaur sculptures in the Crystal Palace grounds at Sydenham (pictured).

Left The Ape of Thoth

Below One of the stone sphinxes guarding a hidden court in Egypt. After falling into disrepair, the whole area has now been restored

Arboretum
Wellingtonia Avenue

Below The Wellingtonia Avenue

Right The Arboretum is a remarkable survivor of the high-Victorian style

Arboretum

The Arboretum is devoted to groups of trees and shrubs intended at least in part for scientific study. The small pool in the south west of the Arboretum is surrounded by varieties of royal fern and tussock grasses.

Wellingtonia Avenue

The avenue was conceived as a formal set piece, in which the Wellingtonia was to dominate. Explorers' accounts of this colossal American tree had aroused great excitement in Europe, and James Bateman was among the first to acquire young plants soon after its introduction into Britain in 1853. He planted them alternately with deodar cedars, which he intended should be removed within twenty years.

Unfortunately, Bateman moved away from Biddulph before he was able to complete his plans; his successor Robert Heath felled the Wellingtonias instead. After years of decline, the remaining trees were felled in 1995, and the whole avenue replanted to the original design. In line with Bateman's original plan, the cedars will be removed over the next few years. On the embanked terraces there are two further ranks of trees: the red chestnuts at the top of the bank set against a dark backdrop of Austrian pines complete Bateman's intended scheme.

Achieving this scheme has not been without its difficulties and in this part of the garden the rising water table and unusual weather conditions have had an adverse affect on some of the trees.

Cherry Orchard
Woodland Terrace

Cherry Orchard

This part of the garden is planted with double morello cherries and other fruit in rows on raised mounds, and pruned uniformly, with cotoneaster clipped into bell shapes below. Beside the path leading from the east terrace to the Wellingtonia Avenue, James Bateman placed pairs of posts connected by chains, up which grew different species of clematis.

Woodland Terrace

This garden was developed in 2007/8 on land that was the site of a hospital ward. This was an area of plantation screening in Bateman's original scheme and the paths have been reinstated on their original footprint. This garden now gives access to the east end of the Geological Gallery. Running along the rendered wall adjacent to the gallery was the orangery, used for the cultivation and display of tender species of plants, although many of these, including Bateman's cherished orchids, continued to be grown in the hot houses at Knypersley.

Left View into the Cherry Orchard in June

Above The newly planted Woodland Terrace

In the restoration of the Woodland Terrace, the National Trust has followed the same approach as it took in the main restoration of the garden. The intention is to create the look and feel of a large, private Victorian garden in its heyday. This approach has been possible because Biddulph excited much attention when it was being laid out and there are very good contemporary accounts written by Edward Kemp and published in *The Gardener's Chronicle*. These included detailed maps of the garden and listings of plants. In the early part of the 20th century, *Country Life* magazine took a series of photographs that have provided a key visual record of the garden in its last days of private ownership. When the National Trust took over the garden in 1988 it commissioned an audit of the plants that had survived and compared these to the lists in *The Gardener's Chronicle*. This enabled a planting list to be drawn up that continues to be used to restore areas of the garden.

Although much of the major restoration work has been completed, a number of areas will require replanting in order to maintain the continuity of trees and shrubs. Wherever possible Biddulph's gardeners propagate from the historic material already in the garden or introduce new plants which are of the period between 1840 and 1870 so as to remain faithful to James Bateman's original vision. Over the years some of the original features in the garden were demolished, such as the music room and the orangery. Together with the Geological Gallery these will form restoration projects over the coming years.

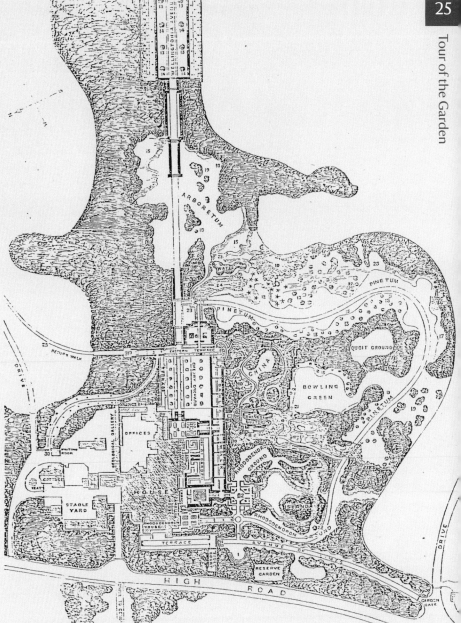

China

This is perhaps the most memorable part of Biddulph and the most famous of its gardens. Completely hidden from the rest of the garden by high banks, trees and walls, it evokes a magical Victorian vision of China. As one emerges from the darkness of the tunnel, a Chinese willow-pattern plate comes to life before your eyes. A path leads to an ornate wooden bridge with a zig-zag fence over a pool beside a temple and surrounded by ornamental trees.

This elaborately theatrical setting was created to display many of the exotic plants that were being brought back from the Far East, especially those discovered by the plant

hunter Robert Fortune: golden larch (Biddulph has one of the oldest surviving golden larches in the country), *Spiraea japonica fortunei* and paulownia. Other particular features are the purple-leaved Japanese maples, Japanese cedars, hostas and tree peonies planted amid tufa, a rock brought from Derbyshire.

The path through China leads past a gigantic frog sitting on the wall, then under a great stone Chinese gateway into a semi-circular space dominated by Benjamin Waterhouse Hawkins's extraordinary sculpture of a Chinese idol in the form of a gilded water buffalo. Below this beast are two gravel-filled parterres cut out of the turf in the shape of dragons. Continuing the theme, James Bateman built a 'Great Wall of China' along the western ridge with the ornamental Joss House perched at one end and a stone watchtower to the north.

The temple, with its adjoining balustraded terrace overlooking the lake, is richly decorated with gilded dragons, sea horses, carved grebes and hanging bells. The multi-coloured roof tiles are copies of the originals and are based on fragments that were discovered in the pool. The building's striking colours are a faithful recreation of the original, although it must be said they bear very little relation to those of an authentic Chinese garden temple.

Below Occupying centre stage is the gilded water buffalo sculpture by Waterhouse Hawkins

The Glen
Dahlia Walk
Araucaria Parterre

The Glen

Having drawn rock formations in Scotland, Edward Cooke combined his artistic and practical landscaping talents to supervise the creation of this outstanding piece of naturalistic rockwork. In the original scheme this Scottish glen was a Himalayan ravine, another area to be represented in James Bateman's world garden.

It was planted with Sikkim and Bhutan rhododendrons, both new to cultivation. Bateman made great efforts to provide ideal growing conditions. Bateman and Cooke shared an enthusiasm for ferns, planting twenty-two different species and cultivars here, together with semi-aquatic plants such as butterwort, and perennials like New Zealand flax and pampas grass.

Dahlia Walk

Bateman shared the Victorians' mania for these bold bedding plants, carving out a generous sunken walk for them through the middle of his garden. Yew hedges divided the terraced beds into a series of compartments in which the strong colours of the dahlia blooms could be shown off to great effect. The Dahlia Walk was later filled in and only rediscovered after excavations in 1988. The beds have been replanted with dahlias similar to the now extinct cultivars that would have been grown at the time.

The Shelter House, which overlooks the Dahlia Walk, is not original but was reconstructed from old photographs and archaeological evidence.

Below left The Glen was restored in the 1980s

Below right Looking down the length of the Dahlia Walk. Each section rises two steps along the length and is divided by clipped yew hedges

Opposite The Araucaria Parterre with the lake and Rhododendron Ground in the background

Araucaria Parterre

The four compartments of the parterre each contain a small Monkey Puzzle Tree. These curious trees are indigenous to the Andes mountain range and are one of the species Bateman and Cooke identified 'living fossils'. This was one of the first parts of the garden to be created. Bateman admired the trees as small specimens and moved them, as they grew too large for his scheme, to the Arboretum. The National Trust continues this tradition to this day.

Mrs Bateman's Garden and Mosaic Parterre

These interconnected and complicated gardens on the top terrace were created in the 1840s but had disappeared by the late 1860s, after the Dahlia Walk was shortened. James Bateman's gardens must originally have been on a series of slopes from west to east following broadly the levels of the Dahlia Walk.

The creation of the terrace walls and the obliteration of the lower part of the Dahlia Walk to make the three broad grassy terraces meant that there was no archaeological evidence of the original designs. The layout, therefore, is an interpretation of Edward Kemp's descriptions.

A faint shadow of the Mosaic Parterre was found, and this has been accurately re-created with crushed terracotta and yellow 'grog' (a by-product of the pottery industry). The other gardens follow the style of Bateman's originals. The furthest west includes iron rose-stands designed precisely to the specification that Bateman recommended in 1858 in one of his few surviving letters to his brother-in-law, Rowland Egerton Warburton of Arley. The planting in these gardens gives a different character at different times of the year, often unusual and sometimes exotic. These are chosen to reflect the style of Maria Bateman, herself a knowledgeable plantswoman and nicknamed the 'Great Lilliophile', providing a clue as to her own tastes in plants. Edward Kemp described the parterres as 'devoted to bulbs, herbaceous plants and any other rare things which individual fancy may select'.

Far left The nanny with four of the Heath children in Mrs Bateman's Garden

Above The lion's head fountain in Mrs Bateman's Garden

Left The Mosaic Parterre

Challenge and Change

Anyone who gardens knows that this is a constantly changing environment and can surely appreciate that working to a 19th-century scheme in the 21st century brings additional challenges. Biddulph was innovative in its day and within a historical context today's garden team strives to meet all challenges.

The work of conserving and restoring the garden is a continuing process that today is in the hands of five gardeners and a dedicated team of volunteers. Today they face challenges that are quite different to those James Bateman encountered when he first arrived at Biddulph. The protection of vistas into and out of the garden is a significant issue as increased urbanization has brought housing developments up to the very edge of the garden. In Bateman's time the views would have been into open countryside. Changing patterns of climate and especially rainfall have also brought new problems to manage in the 21st century.

In their wake, plant diseases affecting yews and rhododendrons in particular have become more commonplace and preventive measures are required to prevent their spread. In some instances this means planting alternative species until the diseases are brought under control.

However, for all the involvement and intervention of our gardeners and volunteers, we hope that if James and Maria Bateman were to pay a visit to the garden today they would find much that is familiar and be pleased with the care taken to restore one of the 19th century's truly outstanding and innovative gardens.